LC:7)18TC5 (6/14)

INTERNET
ADDICTION

INTERNET
ADDICTION

BY LAURA PERDEW

CONTENT CONSULTANT
DR. KEITH W. BEARD
MARSHALL UNIVERSITY
DEPARTMENT OF PSYCHOLOGY

Essential Library

An Imprint of Abdo Publishing | www.abdopublishing.com

www.abdopublishing.com

Published by Abdo Publishing, a division of ABDO, PO Box 398166, Minneapolis, Minnesota 55439. Copyright © 2015 by Abdo Consulting Group, Inc. International copyrights reserved in all countries. No part of this book may be reproduced in any form without written permission from the publisher. Essential Library™ is a trademark and logo of Abdo Publishing.

Printed in the United States of America, North Mankato, Minnesota
042014
092014

Cover Photo: iStockphoto/Thinkstock
Interior Photos: iStockphoto/Thinkstock, 2; DB Dirk Godder/picture-alliance/dpa/ AP Images, 6; Kim Jae-Hwan/AFP/Newscom, 11; Fer Gregory/Shutterstock Images, 14; Susan Sterner/AP Images, 19; Fuse/Thinkstock, 24; Don Heupel/AP Images, 29; Razvan Bucur/Shutterstock Images, 30; Javier Sanchez Mingorance/Thinkstock, 32; Solent News/REX/AP Images, 36; Nigel Treblin/dapd/AP Images, 41; Imaginechina/ AP Images, 45; zeljkodan/Shutterstock Images, 46; Samo Trebizan/Shutterstock Images, 52; Gang Liu/Shutterstock Images, 54; Toby Talbot/AP Images, 56; YanLev/Shutterstock Images, 59; Monkey Business Images/Shutterstock Images, 65; Alliance/Thinkstock, 66; Julie Jacobson/AP Images, 71; CandyBox Images/Shutterstock Images, 75; Peter Cade/Getty Images, 76; kzeno/Thinkstock, 81; Randy Faris/Fuse/Thinkstock, 84; wavebreakmedia/Shutterstock Images, 86; Monkey Business Images/Thinkstock, 90; Stephen Brashear/AP Images, 93

Editor: Angela Wiechmann
Series Designer: Becky Daum

Library of Congress Control Number: 2014932573

Cataloging-in-Publication Data

Perdew, Laura.
 Internet addiction / Laura Perdew.
  p. cm. -- (Essential issues)
Includes bibliographical references and index.
ISBN 978-1-62403-421-3
1. Internet addiction--Juvenile literature. 2. Behavior, addictive--Juvenile literature. I. Title.
616.85--dc23

                                        2014932573

CONTENTS

CHAPTER
ONE

LOST IN THE DIGITAL WORLD

In 2008, Choi Mi-sun—a young, shy South Korean woman—went to a PC bang with her mother. PC bangs, popular in South Korea, are comfortable lounges where users can log on to the Internet for an hourly fee and play whatever virtual games they choose.

Choi visited the PC bang not just to game but also to meet a potential spouse. Eventually she met Kim Yoo-chul online. They were both playing *Prius*, a massively multiplayer online role playing game (MMORPG). The couple spent more and more time online together, met in person, and later married.

After marrying, Choi and Kim still immersed themselves in *Prius*, sometimes up to 12 hours a day. Often they went to an all-night gaming center and did not return until dawn. They belonged to a guild, a cooperative group that worked as a team in the game. They even earned a living selling their game wealth

In wired countries such as South Korea, gamers gather in PC bangs to immerse themselves in online play.

for real money to other gamers. While in their virtual world, the shy, awkward gamers were masters of their own fate, exploring new worlds, staving off monsters, and recovering treasures.

Sarang

In 2009, Choi gave birth to a baby girl they named Sarang. Choi paid little care to her pregnancy. She did not know when the baby was due until she went into labor. The baby was premature and sickly. Even after Sarang was born, the couple continued gaming. Choi and Kim often went as far as to leave their brand-new baby home alone as they lost themselves in the virtual world. In *Prius*, they raised and nurtured a virtual daughter. But their real-life daughter, on the other hand, was often abandoned and fed just twice a day.

Then one day in September, Choi and Kim returned home after a long gaming session to discover Sarang had died. She was only three months old. The couple called emergency services. Once the police arrived, they were immediately suspicious about Sarang's death and how dehydrated she looked. Following Sarang's funeral, Choi and Kim disappeared to avoid the authorities.

The Case

An autopsy revealed Sarang had died of malnutrition. In essence, the baby starved to death. "This constitutes an inhumane crime where the defendants abandoned even the most basic responsibilities as parents, and is unforgivable beyond any excuse or reason," the Suwon District Court said.[2]

CELEBRITY STATUS

South Korean culture is so Internet centered, gamers are considered national celebrities in the same way professional athletes are in other countries. Gaming master Jin Young-Soo has corporate sponsors and fans. He practices countless hours in preparation for big tournaments. His "sport" is *StarCraft*, a real-time military science fiction game. Leading up to a big rematch in 2009, Jin prepared for a year and was confident. Supporters gathered in large groups to watch the tournament live as it was broadcast by two national cable channels. Fans cheered and held their breaths as Jin's opponent launched an offensive. But the nation ultimately lamented Jin's defeat.

The couple was on the run from the law for nearly six months. Finally in March 2010, the police caught up with Choi and Kim and charged them with child abuse and neglect. The couple expressed deep guilt for their daughter's death. They had voluntarily stayed away from gaming in the five months between Sarang's death and the arrest. During the trial, Choi cried and said, "I am sorry for being such a bad mother to my baby."[3]

The prosecution for the case had hoped both Choi and Kim would receive a five-year prison sentence for Sarang's death. However, the defense made a historic claim. For the first time in South Korea, the defense argued Choi and Kim were not responsible for Sarang's death due to their Internet addiction, which impaired their judgment. The claim was that they had been so addicted to the Internet and gaming, they were unaware of their actions in real life. Ultimately the court found them not guilty because Internet addiction was recognized as a mental disorder in South Korea. This cleared Choi and Kim of any responsibility.

The couple no longer participates in gaming. Kim became a taxi driver, and the couple has other children.

With Internet use a nearly universal piece of South Korean culture, the country recognizes Internet addiction as a mental disorder.

Internet Addiction

The prosecution of Choi and Kim was a landmark case worldwide. The ruling could conceivably lay the foundation for an Internet addiction defense for other cases around the world.

South Korea is one of the most wired countries in the world. It boasts the world's highest percentage of Internet users at 82.7 percent, and 78.5 percent of the population uses smartphones.[4] In a study published in October 2013, 99.6 percent of the 15-to-24-year-old group reported actively using the Internet.[5] And on virtually every city street, gamers can find a PC bang.

South Korea puts itself in a position to be one of the first countries to grapple with the concept of Internet addiction and related issues. South Korea has hundreds of facilities for children who have become addicted to gaming. Children are often sent to so-called boot camps and counseling centers to address their addiction.

In April 2011, the South Korean parliament also passed an Internet gaming curfew as a part of the Juvenile Protection Act. The Online Game Shutdown requires gaming centers to restrict access for youth age 16 and younger between midnight and 6:00 a.m. It was intended to curb the growing number of teen

SANDRA HACKER

Before Choi and Kim's case, one of the earliest cases of Internet addiction leading to neglect happened in Ohio in 1997. Sandra Hacker had three children, ages two, three, and five. She also had Internet access in her home at a time when few people did. Hacker apparently became engrossed in the Internet for up to 12 hours at a time, giving little attention to her children. She would lock them in another room while she went online.

The children's father, estranged from his wife, called the child protection agency. When police went into the home, they found broken glass on the floor, feces on the walls, and garbage strewn about. There was hardly any edible food in the refrigerator. In the midst of the filth and squalor, Hacker's computer area was immaculate. The computer itself was worth thousands of dollars.

Hacker was charged with child endangerment, and the children were placed in their father's custody.

gaming addicts in South Korea and underscore the importance of sleep for teens. But netizens were not happy. Opponents of the curfew claim it restricts teens' right to enjoy gaming, which is integral to South Korea's current culture.

Internet addiction is not viewed in the same way in the United States. The American Psychiatric Association (APA) does not recognize Internet addiction as a mental disorder in the fifth edition of its *Diagnostic and Statistical Manual of Mental Disorders* (*DSM-5*), published in 2013. Across its many editions, the *DSM* has been known as the "bible of psychiatry."[6] The only behavioral addiction listed in the *DSM-5* is gambling. Internet Gaming Disorder, however, is listed as a condition in need of more research before it might be added as an identified disorder in future editions of the manual.

Whether recognized officially or unofficially, Internet addiction seems to be affecting lives in the United States and across the globe. Surveys in the United States and Europe indicate as many as 8.2 percent of the population may be affected by compulsive computer use that results in social, psychological, and neurological problems.[7]

CHAPTER
TWO

ORIGINS OF
THE INTERNET

Today the Internet is part of most people's everyday lives. But it has not always been that way. Just after World War II (1939–1945), the common forms of technology and communication in US households were a radio, a record player, and a telephone line.

In the 1950s, television technology use exploded, and by 1960, almost every home in the United States had one. It was the main form of entertainment and source of information. Then in the 1990s, the personal computer began appealing to consumers. In 1994, 24 percent of Americans had a computer. By 2003, the number reached 62 percent.[1] At the same time, the Internet was developing and mobile technology was emerging—a combination that changed the world.

Thanks to the Internet explosion, bulky desktop computers and corded phones are almost relics of the past.

History of the Internet

The Internet was not created by any single person. Instead, it was developed by a number of individuals with the vision and drive to connect people and share information worldwide. As early as the 1930s, Belgian information expert Paul Otlet envisioned using the world's telephone wires and radio waves to create a network. The network he imagined would bring information into people's homes from anywhere in the world. The Internet as people know it today, however, was not conceived until the 1960s. It was developed over time by researchers, computer scientists, engineers, and academics.

Government officials in the Defense Advanced Research Projects Agency (DARPA) wanted to share information between computers. They began a computer project called Advanced Research Projects Agency Network (ARPANET). The basic idea was to share information via common communication lines.

However, researchers discovered sending whole messages over telephone lines would be too slow. To work around this, they developed a system called packet switching that involves breaking a message into little pieces encoded with its destination, or address. Once at the destination, the packets were collected and pieced back together, and the message was delivered. On October 29, 1969, the first computer-to-computer communication was sent, although it made the system crash. Nonetheless, the groundwork had been laid.

Around the same time, programmers at Bell Telephone Laboratories developed a user-friendly operating system called UNIX. It was so successful, most universities in the United States adopted the system as a means to share information within their networks.

In 1977, a small program was added to UNIX that allowed automatic sending of all kinds of data from one machine to another. Initially developed to update software across numerous machines,

E-MAIL

The first e-mails were sent between two computers right next to each other in the same office. In 1971, engineer Ray Tomlinson wanted to communicate with coworkers who would not always answer their telephones. He found a way to send a message between his computer and his colleagues' computers. Thus, e-mail was born. Tomlinson is also responsible for the @ symbol used in e-mail addresses. The purpose of the symbol was to separate the name of the users from the name of their computers. Tomlinson's idea, combined with the growth of networks worldwide, revolutionized the way people communicate.

academics realized its potential to share all kinds of information. Individuals created homemade modems out of telephones and other parts, and they connected their computers via telephone lines. This created Usenet.

Usenet and other networks were integral in popularizing communication between computers. They made computer communication accessible to the general public, when before it was primarily used in government and at universities. In addition, these networks were not under the control of any organization nor were they censored.

January 1, 1983, is officially known as the birthday of the Internet. Before this date, many different networks existed, but they had no way of communicating with each other. In the decade leading up to 1983, researchers had developed the Transmission Control Protocol and Internet Protocol (TCP/IP), which allowed computers on different networks to talk to each other. ARPANET officially switched to the TCP/IP standard on January 1, 1983. From that point forward, a universal language connected all networks.

In the early days of the Internet, computers could communicate only when hardwired in a network.

What Is the Internet?

Connecting computers and sharing information started with a network of users, which led to calling it "the net." Today, the Internet is a network of computers across the globe. But originally, it consisted of connections via cables between a fixed number of computers. Users had to know the routes connecting the computers in order to access or share information.

Tim Berners-Lee, a Briton living in Switzerland, took the net one step further. He developed the idea of "the web." He wanted a simpler way for people to share and access files: data, articles, images, and so on.

The concept of the World Wide Web was introduced to the public in 1990. It made sharing files across the Internet much easier, and it made files available to anyone anywhere in the world.

Berners-Lee also developed icons and buttons still used today to follow links. Browsers and search engines were also created, allowing individuals to search the web for information and to generate links. With these user-friendly additions, web use increased.

All the Rage

In the 1980s, perhaps only graduate student researchers could "surf the net" to access network bulletin boards, chat rooms, and the like. But once the Internet became accessible to the general public in 1990, its popularity exploded.

In the 1990s, the Internet used dial-up technology via telephone lines. Although revolutionary at the time, it was also slow, especially compared to today's standards. The birth of broadband connections and wireless capabilities made Internet access quicker and more versatile. With faster access, people increasingly turned to the Internet to search for information and communicate. In 1997, the US Census Bureau reported

18 percent of homes used the Internet. By 2003, that number had more than tripled to 55 percent.[2] In 2011, 71.7 percent of US households used the Internet.[3] People were hooked on the ease and accessibility of digital technology.

Mobile Technology

Accessing the Internet on computers was just the beginning. The first mobile phone call was made in

DEMOGRAPHICS OF INTERNET USE

Who uses the Internet in the United States? To some degree, everyone does, but there are some differences in Internet use across demographics such as age, education level, and income. As of September 2013, 98 percent of adults 18 to 29 reported using the Internet, compared to 59 percent of those 65 and older. Men and women were about equal in their use.

The more educated people are, the more likely they are to access the Internet. That is, 97 percent of college graduates use the Internet, compared to 56 percent of those who did not graduate high school.[4]

Income is likewise correlated. The greater one's income, the more likely he or she is to use the Internet.

Among teens 12 to 17, 95 percent reported using the Internet in 2012. Interestingly, while income and education has a major effect on adults' Internet usage, parental income and education has only a minor effect on teens' Internet use. For example, when parents' income is less than $30,000, 89 percent of teens report using the Internet. When the parents' income is above $75,000, the amount is 99 percent. This perhaps illustrates how nearly all children in the modern world are growing up connected.[5]

New York City on April 3, 1973. The call was made on a device weighing 3.3 pounds (1.5 kg). A decade later in 1984, Motorola released the first mobile phone for public consumers. That phone weighed 1.8 pounds (0.8 kg).[6] Today's smartphones weigh approximately 0.25 pounds (112 g) yet have more computing power than the *Apollo 11* space shuttle.[7]

Since 2006, the cell phone has topped the list of technology ownership. Computer ownership is actually second to cell phones. By May 2013, 91 percent of adults in the United States owned a cell phone. Furthermore, three out of every five phones were smartphones.[8]

On December 3, 1992, Neil Papworth sent the first text message. The 22-year old sent a message from his large computer to a friend's mobile phone. His friend could not return the message because at the time cell phones were not equipped for messaging. A year later, Nokia came out with the first cell phone with the capability to send messages.

By 2007, people were sending 28.9 billion texts every month in the United States. The number reached 184.3 billion by 2012.[9] Among cell phone owners, 81 percent use them to send and receive text messages, but phones are also used to search for information, send e-mail, access music, and more.[10]

Since the 1990s, the explosion of technology has produced new mobile gadgets seemingly every day. In 2006, the majority of adults owned desktop computers, but since then, laptop ownership has surpassed desktop ownership. E-book readers and tablets are also popular, both of which offer Internet access.

With the growth of mobile devices, more and more people are connecting to the Internet wirelessly. By August 2011, 63 percent of American adults went online with their mobile devices.[11]

As a result of the technology revolution, people are picking up more gadgets and connecting in new ways—and spending increasingly more time on the Internet. But for some, this increased use can lead to an addiction.

MOBILE TEENS

At the Pew Research Center, researcher Mary Maddens believes teens in the United States are on the cutting edge of mobile technology. The center's March 2013 study shows many teens ages 12 to 17 no longer use Internet connections from a family desktop or laptop computer. Of the 95 percent of teenagers who use the Internet, 25 percent report connecting almost exclusively via their own cell phones.[12] Today's teens are always "on," staying wirelessly connected using mobile devices.

CHAPTER
THREE

INTERNET ADDICTION EMERGES

In today's digital world, there seems to be a thin line between technology use and abuse. Many people's Internet habits may seem excessive: sleeping with a smartphone under the pillow, texting one person while having a face-to-face conversation with another, or tweeting from a funeral. But some people cross that thin line even one step further, going from Internet use and abuse to Internet addiction.

New Technology, New Addiction

The first person to publically use the phrase "Internet addiction disorder" meant it as a joke. In 1995, psychiatrist Ivan Goldberg posted a humorous entry about Internet addiction on PsyCom.net. He crafted it to read like an entry in the *DSM*. In his post, Goldberg

In the technology age, the distinction between Internet use and abuse can be unclear.

25

described symptoms such as "a need for markedly increased amounts of time on Internet to achieve satisfaction" and "involuntary typing movements of the fingers."[1]

Goldberg meant it all in jest, but many people thought he was describing a real condition. Perhaps this was because real people were having real problems with the newly emerging Internet. While Goldberg may have been joking, other professionals began seriously questioning whether there may in fact be such a disorder as Internet addiction.

As an assistant professor of psychology at the University of Pittsburgh at Bradford, Kimberly Young presented her findings in 1996. She argued a new disorder was emerging with this new form of technology. She likened Internet addiction to other

WHAT IS NORMAL?

In order to define whether someone's Internet usage is abnormal or addictive, one must first determine "normal" use. This is challenging because technology use has increased over the years. In the 1990s, for example, the Internet was so new, there was no true baseline for use. In 1997, the 20 million regular netizens in the United States surfed the net only "once a week or so." Average use of the Internet at the time was eight hours a week.[2] By today's standards, these figures are incredibly low. "Normal" use keeps changing, making it difficult to scientifically classify Internet addiction as a disorder.

impulse-control disorders. Using gambling addiction as a model, Young generated questions to help other professionals assess Internet addiction. She also opened the Center for Internet Addiction in 1995.

Since then, many researchers have studied compulsive use of the Internet. Supporting Young's conclusions, Mark Griffiths of the United Kingdom saw the similarities between Internet addiction and other addictive behaviors. Some doctors as well began noting physical symptoms associated with Internet addiction. These include carpal tunnel syndrome, dry eyes, migraines, back aches, poor eating habits, poor hygiene, and irregular sleep. This supported the notion that Internet addiction, like other addictions, creates physical consequences and other problems in individuals' lives.

Defining Addiction

In medical terms, an addiction is a "habitual compulsion to engage in a certain activity or utilize a substance, notwithstanding the devastating consequences on the individual's physical, social, spiritual, mental, and financial well-being."[3] In simpler terms, addicts crave a substance or experience and get a rush from engaging in it. People's lives become centered on the addictive behavior. Health and emotional problems arise. This can include ignoring one's health, family, and finances.

From a neurological perspective, the basis of any addiction is the rush the brain receives. During enjoyable activities, people experience a flood of the neurotransmitter dopamine, which activates the pleasure centers of the brain. Dopamine is the brain's reward for engaging in certain activities. When the activity is repeated with the same pleasurable outcomes, the behavior is reinforced. This means the brain wants to do it again and again, and an addiction can form.

When the behavior becomes an addiction, the brain constantly craves that dopamine rush. In time, individuals develop tolerance. This means they must increase the duration or intensity of the behavior in order to produce the same rush. The cycle continues, and addicts must engage in the behavior more. And when the brain does not get its rush, an individual experiences anxiety and other withdrawal symptoms. Now the person is driven to repeat the behavior not only to get the rush, but also to alleviate the adverse effects of withdrawal.

Studies have shown some Internet users experience these elevated levels of dopamine, just as a drug or

Kimberly Young was among the first to recognize an addiction arising from the new Internet technology of the 1990s.

substance addict would. Users get a rush or high from their online activities. For Internet addicts, being online becomes the most important part of their lives. The Internet consumes thoughts, behaviors, and feelings. But then users begin to need increasingly more time online to get the same high. When they cannot be online, Internet addicts suffer withdrawal symptoms. They also tend to be at risk for relapses, even after years of having their Internet use under control.

The thrill of the Internet is similar to the thrill of a slot machine.

Like a Slot Machine

The Internet provides a particular type of reinforcement that makes it quite addictive to some people. As David Greenfield, founder of the Center for Internet and Technology Addiction, explains, "The whole Internet operates on a variable ratio reinforcement schedule."[4] This means the Internet is similar to a slot machine at a casino.

When people play slot machines, they never know what will happen with each turn. They will either lose money or make money. If they do win, the payout varies. Perhaps it will be enough to cover the next turn. Or perhaps it will be a big jackpot. This sense of the unknown builds excitement. If and when players do win big, it produces a rush—and it keeps them playing, craving that next payout.

Internet addicts crave and seek out many different rushes online. The Internet "payout" is variable and unpredictable. When people go online, they never know when they will hit a "jackpot." They do not know when a great post, e-mail, or sale will come in, where it will come from, or what it will be. Therefore, like playing a slot machine, the connection to technology is reinforced in exciting and unpredictable ways.

Emotional Cravings

But there is more to the Internet than the thrill of the unknown. Some users also find themselves addicted to the Internet for emotional reasons. A number of addicts rely on the Internet because they feel unable to connect with others in person. They find much-needed community in cyberspace. Individuals can join multiplayer games, chat, text, e-mail, keep up with friends on social networking sites, find people to date, and more. The Internet allows people to rewrite the

Many people are drawn to the Internet because it helps them shape their identity.

rules of interaction—controlling the when, where, who, and how. That can be a rush for people who have trouble with the conventions and limitations of face-to-face interaction.

Still others crave the Internet as a means to escape or avoid stressful events in their real lives. They can create a new sense of reality. When life is seemingly out of control, going online gives some people a temporary sense of power. They can choose whom to "friend" or "defriend." They can conquer games. They can buy whatever they want whenever they want it. If an online interaction becomes uncomfortable, they can just log off. Other addicts crave the anonymity of the Internet, feeling it gives them power to say or do things they might never consider offline. This is called disinhibition.

Another allure for some Internet addicts is the ability to adopt a different personality or identity. This holds true for gamers with avatars as well as people with profiles on social networking sites. In both situations, the Internet allows people to represent themselves in new or seemingly better ways. Some people lose

CYBERBULLYING

Some bullies confront their targets at school or on the street. But in the digital age, cyberbullies can send harassing messages anytime, anywhere, and to anyone.

Cyberbullying may be a form of disinhibition. The Cyberbullying Research Center defines cyberbullying as "when someone repeatedly harasses, mistreats, or makes fun of another person online or while using cell phones or other electronic devices."[5] In a 2010 study, the center found more than 20 percent of students had been bullied in this manner.[6]

According to experts, the Internet reinforces and intensifies bullies' motives because it provides distance and anonymity. That is, some bullies are more malicious online than in person. Similarly, bullies may think they have a great deal of power in cyberspace, especially if the Internet hides their identities.

In addition, the threat of punishment or social consequences is greatly reduced online. A bully may not be bold enough to harass another student in a crowded hallway full of other students and teachers. But online, the bully knows the only witness is often the victim.

themselves online. That is, they lose control of their behavior and also lose their true sense of identity.

Not Recognized

While many experts insist Internet addiction is a legitimate mental disorder, that belief is not universally held in the industry. Most notably, the APA does not officially recognize it in the *DSM-5*. A disorder's inclusion in the *DSM* plays a significant role for those seeking treatment, such as whether treatment may be covered by insurance. This means individuals with Internet addiction may face different financial responsibilities than people with drug or gambling addictions face when receiving treatment.

Some mental health professionals support the APA's decision to not recognize Internet addiction as a disorder. These experts claim an Internet addiction diagnosis is unscientific. Psychologist John Grohol, frequent critic of Internet addiction, states overusing the Internet is no worse than reading books all the time or watching too much television. In addition, opponents argue excessive Internet use may be a symptom of other underlying issues, such as depression or anxiety. These deeper issues, they claim, are the real mental disorders that require treatment.

Despite these opposing views, many professionals are working to establish Internet addiction as a disorder in its own right. To this end, experts cite parallels between Internet addiction and other forms of addiction. They point out how standards defining other recognized disorders, especially gambling addiction, can be easily applied to Internet addiction. They also cite how Internet addiction results in serious consequences to one's well-being. Greenfield has seen the impact since the late 1990s, stating, "Marriages are being disrupted, kids are getting into trouble, people are committing illegal acts, people are spending too much money."[7]

THE CHEMISTRY OF ADDICTION

Some experts question whether Internet addiction is a matter of chemistry or behavior. In the medical field, doctors classify an addiction as a chemical disorder. Drug use, therefore, can lead to addiction because it changes the brain's chemistry. From this view, so-called Internet addiction is an impulse-control problem because it affects only behavior.

In contrast, professionals in the mental health field argue that behaviors can become addictions in the fullest sense. They note that behaviors, such as Internet use, can produce a rush of dopamine. The brain reacts not unlike it would to a drug, with cravings, withdrawal, and increasing tolerance.

CHAPTER
FOUR

GAMING

The first known video game was *Noughts and Crosses*. It was a ticktacktoe game developed by a Cambridge University student as part of his doctoral dissertation in 1952. In the new millennium, video games are the primary source of entertainment for hundreds of millions of people worldwide. Among youths in the United States, 83 percent own video game consoles.[1]

But while gaming is merely entertainment for most people, it can develop into an addiction for others. The APA included Internet Gaming Disorder in its "Conditions for Further Study" section of the *DSM-5*. Of all the behaviors people engage in online, gaming seems to have an especially addictive quality. The *DSM-5* states that when people play games, "certain pathways in their brains are triggered in the same direct and intense way that a drug addict's brain is affected by a particular substance."[2]

Online gaming is more than just entertainment for some—it's a way of life.

Captivating Games

Since 1952, games have evolved dramatically, from arcade machines to Atari games to MMORPGs. In the modern world, games are only a click away on any Internet-ready device: computers, game consoles, handheld consoles, tablets, smartphones, and more.

There are countless games, with something for every age and every interest. There are puzzle games and physical games. Interactive educational games are sometimes used in the classroom. Simulation, or sim games, let people manage and control an online world. The list goes on to include adventure games, sports games, first-person shooter games, real-time strategy games, role-playing games (RPGs), and MMORPGs.

Across all categories, companies specifically design their online games to be captivating. Developers build what are called hooks into the games to ensure people will keep playing. Designers often hook players by making games challenging but not impossible to win. Many gamers crave the sense of accomplishment and reward as they advance to the next level or solve difficult puzzles. The sense of achievement can boost their self-esteem. In the same vein, a major hook is a scoring system. In many games, players get a rush when they beat their previous high score or someone else's. Or they will continue playing until they earn a perfect score.

MMORPGs

MMORPGs are immensely popular, and they tend to be the most addictive type of game. In games such as *World of Warcraft* (*WoW*), players enter a fantasy world and interact with other online players around the world. MMORPGs hook gamers because they are quite immersive. They allow for unpredictable discovery as a story unfolds in imaginary worlds, and there is no end or winning. Some people lose themselves in the endless sense of discovery.

Like many types of games, MMORPGs allow players to create avatars, or digital selves,

GAMIFICATION

Games have hooks, and now some jobs do too. Many corporations integrate addictive game components into the workplace to motivate employees. Game elements can increase productivity, satisfaction, and innovation. At Microsoft, for example, workers testing for program bugs now receive "points" when they solve problems.

Adam Penenberg's *Play At Work: How Games Inspire Breakthrough Thinking* takes a look at "gamification" in the world today.[3] He believes companies will increasingly use game applications for training, marketing, and performance because games are so popular and have been proven effective. Penenberg even predicts companies will eventually turn entire jobs into games.

with customized physical and personal characteristics. Avatars frequently represent the identity a gamer wishes to be or wants to experiment with. In MMORPGs, many players form emotional attachments to their avatars. They find it difficult to stop playing because of that connection.

But that is not the only connection gamers make. Another strong hook for MMORPGs is the sense of relationship and community players can develop online. For some, the online world is the first or only place they feel accepted. Sometimes players create guilds, and they embark on quests together. These online bonds are deep for many people.

With so many hooks in MMORPGs, some gamers immerse themselves to the point of addiction. The real world gives way too easily to the online world. In response

World of Warcraft is one of the most popular—
and perhaps most addictive—MMORPGs.

to the accusation that *WoW* actually promotes gaming addiction, the makers of the game said, "Our ultimate goal as a game company has always been to make the best games that we can possibly make." But they did add a word of caution: "With any form of entertainment, we feel it's important to exercise personal responsibility and be mindful of outside obligations."[5]

The Effects of Gaming Addiction

Connor, a 17-year old, was performing poorly in school despite his high IQ. He was frequently tired and irritable. He sometimes fell asleep in class. Concerned about his behavior, Connor's mother eventually discovered he was staying up all night playing *WoW*. When she confronted Connor, he admitted to his all-night gaming and said he wanted to stop.

Connor's story reveals some of the consequences when an interest in online games turns into an addiction. Performance drops at work and school. For many gamers, the virtual world usually takes precedent over anything IRL, which is gaming lingo for "in real life." This can lead to social isolation. Real-life relationships with friends and family are often neglected, sometimes to the point where the relationships are irreparably damaged. In fact, among married gamers, up to 50 percent admit their online addiction causes a strain in their marriages. For teens, the lack of social interaction means they will not develop social skills as they turn down chances to interact face-to-face.

Frequently, gaming addicts also suffer physical symptoms. Carpal tunnel syndrome can occur when gamers overuse their hands on game controllers, causing irritation or swelling in their wrists. Some chronic gamers also experience migraines, vision problems, and back pain. The gaming lifestyle likewise leads to poor eating habits, sleep deprivation, and poor hygiene. It leaves little time for healthier activities.

Another concern about prolonged exposure to video games is the increased likelihood gamers will take

UNCLE SAM WANTS GAMERS

Jake was a 21-year-old who lived with his mother and had a gaming addiction. Jake was a slacker, not able to keep a job. Gaming controlled his life. Then one day on an impulse, Jake walked into a US Army recruitment center. After admitting his history with gaming, Jake was surprised by the recruiter's response: "You're perfect for the Army."[6] As it turned out, the games Jake played were similar to the battlefield tracking system the army uses. Many soldiers were previous gamers, turning their addictions into assets.

Since 2004, the army has used video games as a training and recruitment tool. The navy is now doing the same. Larry McCracken, a navy captain, says, "The realism you get is the ability to keep somebody engaged and play a game for two or three or four hours as opposed to in a classroom, where after 15 minutes they're bored."[7] In fact, game developers are now seeing the US military as a new target market, designing games specifically for it.

improper and dangerous risks. Researchers found that among all forms of media, video games glorifying risk taking—such as binge drinking and street racing—were the most likely to prompt risky behaviors in real life.

Breaking the Habit

People addicted to gaming simply feel they cannot stop. One mother tried to get help for her son's gaming addiction, and the only advice people could give her was to merely limit his playing time. "They didn't understand that I couldn't," she said. "He had lost touch with reality . . . the game was the only thing that mattered to him."[8]

But there is hope. In September 2013, former gamer Cam Adair spoke at a conference in Colorado. He talked candidly about his ten-year video game addiction. He dropped out of high school at 15. His parents urged him to get a job, but Adair lied to them. In the mornings, Adair's father would drop him off at the supposed workplace. After his father drove away, Adair would sneak back home to sleep all day because he stayed up gaming all night.

Adair admitted, "I didn't want to do these things. . . . The addiction controlled the behavior."

Gaming addicts often find themselves trapped in the virtual world and unable to cope in the real world.

Despite the shame, guilt, and depression, he continued playing. He reached a point, however, when he knew he needed to quit. And he did—cold turkey. Adair ended his conference address by saying that sometimes all addicts need is permission to move on, to get out of the trap. And to addicted gamers who want to quit, Adair said, "You have permission."[9]

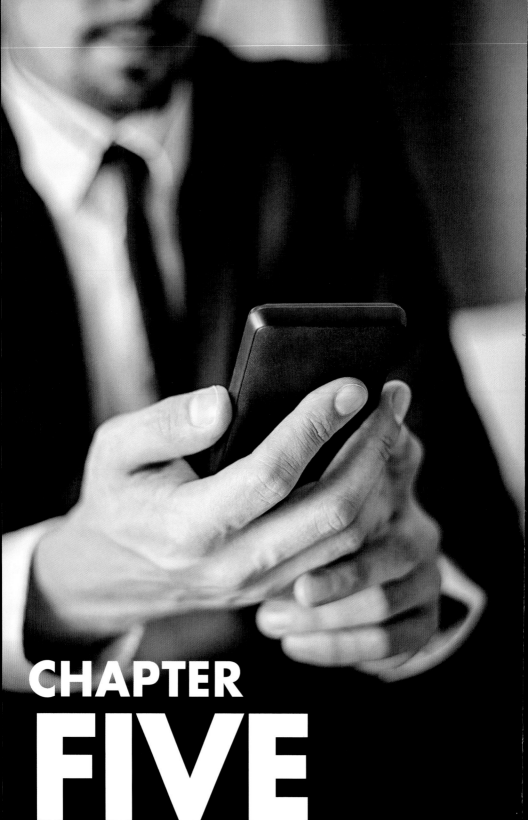

CHAPTER
FIVE

COMMUNICATING

The first telegraph was sent in 1837. From that point, communication forms have accelerated at lightning speed and in unprecedented ways. Thanks to the boom of wireless Internet, communication is now instantaneous and ongoing—at stores, in classrooms, in restaurants, anywhere. Whether calling, e-mailing, or texting, people can connect with others constantly, no matter where they are. But that unlimited access is exactly what can drive some people to the point of addiction.

Cell Phones and Smartphones

The line between dependency and addiction can be thin, especially when it comes to today's phones. One 14-year-old girl, in typical teen-speak, said she spends "like half the day" on her phone.[1] Even adults echo her sentiments. "If I don't have it on me, I feel like I'm not in control or in charge of my life," one woman said of her phone. Another claimed, "All day long, from the minute

Internet communication, such as texting, is an integral part of daily life.

I wake up until I shut it off at night and go to sleep I'm on the phone constantly."[2]

Cell phones and especially smartphones seem indispensable. Aside from making phone calls, owners tend to use cell phones primarily for text messaging. Other uses include accessing the Internet, sending and receiving e-mails, downloading and using apps, and finding information. Teens use their phones similarly to adults, but they tend to send more photos and videos as well as play and record music.

In a 2012 survey, 29 percent of participants described their phones as something they cannot live without.[3] Many others admitted feeling anxious without their phones. People feel the need to check their phones often: one in four admit to checking it at least every 30 minutes.[4] More so, young adults ages 18 to 30 check their

LOL

From texting to e-mailing to instant messaging, online communication is practically its own language. As the Internet has evolved for years without a governing body, netizens have created their own language and lingo. For faster, easier communication online, people rely on acronyms such as LOL for "laughing out loud" and emoticons such as a colon and a parenthesis to indicate a happy face. Beyond the language itself, users have developed online rules and etiquette. This unwritten netiquette defines how people should communicate when online. For example, it is poor netiquette to e-mail in all caps, which is considered the equivalent of shouting.

smartphones at least once every 10 minutes.[5] And 67 percent of adults admit to checking their phones even if they have not rung or vibrated.[6]

Greenfield addresses the line between abuse and addiction when it comes to phones and communication. In today's world, he admits many people probably abuse technology to the extent where the technology interferes in one's life in small ways. Addiction, however, is when the use of technology interferes in major ways—to the point where it affects school, jobs, home life, and relationships.

One example of abuse blurring into addiction is the increased level of anxiety addicts feel without their phones. One survey reported 70 percent of women

PHANTOM VIBRATION SYNDROME

Can checking one's phone even without it ringing or vibrating be a sign of an addiction? According to Larry Rosen, author of *iDisorder*, it may just be. It even has a name: phantom vibration syndrome. Rosen states:

I think it's a fascinating phenomenon. I think it comes . . . from anxiety. Our body is always in waiting to anticipate any kind of technological interaction, which usually comes from a smartphone. With that anticipatory anxiety, if we get any neurological stimulation, our pants rubbing against our leg for example, you might interpret that through the veil of anxiety, as "Oh, my phone is vibrating."[7]

and 61 percent of men experienced separation anxiety without their phones.[8]

But at a more extreme level is the newly described condition of nomophobia. The word *nomophobia* is a shortened form of "no mobile phone."[9] Nomophobics have become so addicted to their phones they have a debilitating fear of being without them. When they are without their phones or service, nomophobics experience symptoms similar to chemical withdrawal.

Texting

Especially for teenage digital natives, texting is the primary way to communicate. Teens seem to crave texting because phones are small, portable, and private—and rarely monitored by parents. Teens can be excessively drawn to texting because it is nonverbal, secretive, and all but coded. The number of text messages teens send and receive has steadily increased since the first one was sent in 1992. By 2011, teens ages 14 to 17 averaged 100 texts per day.[10]

But once again, some people cross the line into addiction. They crave texting to the point where they experience withdrawal symptoms without the rush each message brings. Researchers studying the patterns of addictive phone use have noted a condition they call text-message dependency. Studied mostly with young people in highly wired Asian countries, text-message dependency has symptoms such as sleeping with one's phone to never miss an incoming message. Further, text-message dependency leads youths to exhibit anxiety when they are without their phones. The condition is not unique to Asian teens, however. In the United States, even 44 percent of adults admit to sleeping with their phones nearby for around-the-clock texting.[11]

SEXTING

As cell phone ownership becomes nearly universal, there is growing concern about how the technology is being used. Some people are using their phones in the most personal of ways. Sexting, as defined by Pew Internet, is "sending, receiving, or forwarding suggestive photos or videos of oneself or another person using one's cell phone." In a 2010 study, 6 percent of adults reported sending such a message themselves, and 15 percent of cell phone owners reported receiving one. In a survey in 2009, even teens 12 to 17 reported similar statistics.[12] Some teens in the study claimed sexting is simply part of being in an intimate relationship.

But many people of all ages do not realize the consequences of sending material into cyberspace, where it can be forwarded at will. Further, posting or forwarding sexts can lead to serious legal consequences.

Sleeping with a cell phone nearby could be a possible symptom of Internet addiction.

Effects of Phone Addiction

At Kent State, researchers were curious about the effects of excessive smartphone use. They surveyed undergraduate students about their phone use, grade point average (GPA), anxiety level, and overall happiness. The results, published in 2013, revealed that students with high cell phone use had lower GPAs, higher levels of anxiety, and lower levels of satisfaction with life, compared to students who used their phones less frequently. In another study, Kent State researchers also found a correlation between high cell phone use and poor cardiorespiratory fitness.

These findings have significant implications for people addicted to cell phone use and other forms of online communication. Like any addiction, cell phone addiction can likely lead to physical, social, and emotional problems. Sleep patterns are disrupted when people put their phones next to their beds or under their pillows at night. Excessive texting can create tendon problems in users' thumbs or other problems with their hands and fingers. And still others neglect proper nutrition when consumed by the constant influx of digital communication.

An excessive reliance on texting and e-mailing also impacts overall communication skills. Adman Omar, an information systems expert, found that teens who typically communicate online are less proficient with language, use a smaller vocabulary, and are less expressive. In casual e-mail and texts, simple communication is acceptable. However, it does not meet the standards of communication most people need to succeed in school and careers. Addicts, especially, may see long-term consequences from overusing such methods of communication.

Digital natives often miss out on much-needed face-to-face interaction.

An overreliance on online communication has social implications as well. When asked why he preferred electronic communication, a 23-year-old said, "Talking face-to-face is harder because you have to keep eye contact and give them your attention."[13] But psychologist Sheryl Turkle emphasizes that face-to-face interactions are important in ways e-mailing, texting, and even talking on the phone cannot replicate. Face-to-face conversations are opportunities for negotiating, understanding emotional cues, handling confrontation, and dealing with emotions.

As a result, Turkle believes people who are too connected to digital communication are likely not making real, emotional connections. Socially awkward people may find themselves in a vicious cycle when their behavior turns to addiction. The more uncomfortable they are communicating in person, the more they crave online communication. But the more they turn to online communication, the more uncomfortable they are in person.

CHAPTER
SIX

SOCIAL NETWORKING

Human beings are social animals. Therefore, Internet geologist Susannah Fox says the rise of social networking should not be a surprise. In the modern world, online social networks can broaden a sense of community and increase conversation. Technology has changed what it means to be social and has reshaped how people experience community. As with other online activities, however, it can also turn into an addiction.

A Virtual Social Life

Especially among digital natives, social networking sites are an integral part of interacting with others. Social networking sites such as Facebook give users an online platform to connect and build relationships with other people. Often people connect through shared interests and backgrounds. Some people network with family,

Social networking sites such as Facebook have revolutionized how people connect.

friends, and others they know personally. But the Internet also allows users to make new connections with people across the globe.

In 2013, 73 percent of online adult Americans used social networking sites. Specifically, young adults ages 18 to 29 were the highest users at 90 percent.[1] For teens ages 12 to 17, 95 percent are online, and of those, 76 percent report using social networking sites.[2]

Founded on February 4, 2004, Facebook is perhaps the most popular social networking site. As long ago as 2011, people spent a whopping 700 billion minutes on Facebook every month. Every day, users installed more than 20 million apps and uploaded in excess of 100 billion photographs.[3] And the site's popularity has only continued growing since.

SHARING TOO MUCH

More than ever, teens are sharing personal information on social networking sites. In 2013, Pew Internet reported 92 percent of teens use their real names on their profiles. In addition, 91 percent reported posting photos of themselves online. More than 70 percent share the names of their schools and the towns they live in.[4] Many teens post their e-mail addresses or phone numbers. Even riskier, some teens share sensitive passwords with friends.

The more information individuals share, the more they put themselves at risk for identity theft and impersonation. Worse yet, it can make them vulnerable to predatory criminals and endanger their personal safety.

Social networking sites make it easy for users to post photos and share updates of every moment of their lives.

There are many other popular social media sites in addition to Facebook. Pinterest has been rising in popularity, with a 1,000 percent increase in use from 2011 to 2012. Blogger, Twitter, WordPress, and LinkedIn are also among the top choices. In 2013, Pew Internet reported that Instagram, a site for sharing photos, was also popular. Many adults spend time on Twitter. A 2012 Pew Internet report found there were 225 million Twitter followers at that time, with almost 20 million keeping up with 60 or more Twitterers.[5]

Some experts assert these social networking opportunities can be quite positive, when taken in moderation. Journalist Clive Thompson sees it as a way for people to connect to others' lives in unprecedented ways. He believes updates and snippets of information may be insignificant on their own, but when "taken together, over time, the little snippets coalesce into a surprisingly sophisticated portrait of your friends' and family members' lives."[6] It all adds up to a certain amount of intimacy, he remarks.

Likewise, others believe social networking sites are nothing new when it comes to creating and maintaining friendships. People have always had close friends and also acquaintances. The only difference, some experts contend, is that people now reinforce their relationships

SHARING LIVES

A major piece of social networking is sharing photos and videos on sites such as YouTube. As of 2013, 54 percent of Internet users had posted photos or videos online. Among young adults, that number was 81 percent.

When not taken to an extreme, this type of sharing can be positive. "Sharing photos and videos online adds texture, play, and drama to people's interactions in their social networks," said Pew Internet's Maeve Duggan. "Pictures document life from a special angle. . . . This all adds up to a new kind of collective digital scrapbook with fresh forms of storytelling and social bonding."[7]

online. Social networking can become problematic, however, when people go too far.

How Social Networks Become Addictive

For many users, social networking sites are admittedly a huge distraction, consuming hours of attention a day. And for others, the sites go from being distractions to addictions. One 19-year-old college student said, "I check Facebook at least ten times a day. I have to admit that even when I'm in class, I have Facebook open. It is totally addicting."[8]

Social networking provides users with a quick thrill, like any other addiction. With Twitter, for example, some people feel a short-term rush of self-worth as they gain more followers. The brain then craves those addictive pleasure hits, causing the individual to tweet even more. But eventually, addicts become completely consumed with composing new tweets and gaining more followers in order to maintain that rush. Some begin to neglect their real lives in favor of their virtual community, as the social networking becomes all-consuming. They will turn down an invitation to go out with friends just so they can stay home and catch up with their "friends" online.

Stunting Real-World Social Skills

Turkle believes technology connects people but simultaneously keeps them apart. Some people crave the online connections they perhaps cannot find in real life. Turkle claims sites such as Facebook or Twitter allow people a platform in a world where they often feel no one is listening. As she explained,

> Technology appeals to us most where we are most vulnerable. And we are vulnerable. We're lonely, but we're afraid of intimacy. And so from social networks to sociable robots, we're designing technologies that will give us the illusion of companionship without the demands of friendship.[9]

But when people socialize only through the Internet, they lack face-to-face interaction—the combined acts of speaking, listening, and observing body language. For youths, this often stunts social and verbal skills, making them feel awkward around others. This in turn leads some teens to withdraw from real-life social situations. It creates a pattern where the addict needs online socializing all the more.

Some people favor online socializing because they think it gives them control. Technology allows people to manage how much time they spend with one another. In contrast, face-to-face conversations can be unpredictable. People can rarely control where the conversation goes and how long it takes. But in cyberspace, individuals can plan what they are going to say and edit before they send it. However, Turkle warns this controlled approach does not "really work

ONLINE DATING

At one time before the Internet boom, online dating seemed like an odd concept. Dating sites were met with criticism when they first emerged. Some people thought online dating was too casual and impersonal, compared to traditional methods of mingling and dating face-to-face.

But more and more singles have turned to the Internet to find their mates. In fact, in 2013, 10 percent of Americans reported having used online dating sites. Of those, 23 percent met spouses or partners through the sites. Popular sites include Match.com and eHarmony.

Some people use dating sites to connect with singles they then meet in person. Others have video dates, connecting on-screen. And still others have virtual dates through avatars, which combine dating with gaming.

With online dating becoming more common over the years, most people now view it positively. Of the online daters in the 2013 study, 79 percent believed it was a good way to meet people, and 70 percent believed the sites helped match people.[10]

Whether in the real world or online, dating sometimes has its downsides. A common issue with online dating is that some people create profiles that misrepresent themselves.

for learning about each other, for really coming to know and understand each other."[11]

Taking a Break

More and more teens, especially, are recognizing the negative effects of addictive social networking. Turkle has helped many young people looking to disengage with Facebook and other social networks. Some of these teens saw their real-life relationships suffer while they cultivated their online "friends." Other teens felt too much real-world pressure from their virtual-world profiles.

As an example, Turkle referenced one 18-year-old boy who depicted a glowing, overachieving version of himself for college applications. "Facebook wasn't merely a distraction . . . it was really confusing him about who he was," Turkle said. "He was burned out . . . trying to live up to his own descriptions of himself."[12]

In response, some teens deactivated their accounts. Others took a break. Either way, a lot of self-control was involved. For many, once they made the decision to take a break or take down their profiles, the result was relief.

Some young people are overwhelmed trying to live up to
the identity they create in their Facebook profiles.

CHAPTER
SEVEN

SHOPPING AND GAMBLING

People shopped and gambled long before the Internet. However, the Internet enables these behaviors in new ways. It is easy to see how addictions can develop.

Most notably, the Internet offers anytime, anywhere accessibility. Shoppers and gamblers no longer need to go to stores and casinos. People now have access to these activities any time of the day or night, all from the comfort of home. The Internet provides immediate excitement with the rush of winning or buying, which encourages continued behavior. Online shopping and gambling also give addicts a sense of anonymity and an illusion of control. Using mobile devices, shoppers and gamblers can hide their behavior from others. The cycle continues.

An addiction to online shopping and gambling can send users down the road to financial ruin.

Shopaholics

Darleen was a 33-year-old mother of four and small-business owner. Before picking up her son from preschool, she would pull her car over for a daily fix. Her high was online shopping. Once she started the habit, she could not stop. For a while, packages arrived at her house every single day. Darleen's credit card bills started totaling more than $2,000 per month. Darleen says, "It was so easy to lose track of how much I was spending."[1]

For many people, shopping is a fun hobby—they just like to shop. They like to buy the latest and greatest gadgets or the newest fashions. But many Americans are truly addicted to shopping, the majority of them women. According to the *American Journal of Psychiatry*, between 2 and 5 percent of Americans have a shopping problem.[2]

Shopping addicts often purchase items they do not need or cannot afford. Sometimes they even purchase items they do not use. For addicts, a purchase is all about the rush. Shopping provides a temporary high. The impulse becomes irresistible, despite the impact on one's career, relationships, or finances.

Online shopping is not the same sensory experience as shopping in a store. Online, people cannot feel the fabrics, test the gadgets, and so on. But 24-7 Internet access nevertheless makes feeding the addiction easy.

AMAZON.COM

Amazon.com opened for business on July 16, 1995. It was headquartered in a two-car garage in Bellevue, Washington. A couple employees packed books into boxes on a table made out of an old door.

Amazon.com launched on the cusp of a revolutionary cultural shift. The Internet was new, as was the idea of shopping without being able to actually touch items. Amazon.com and other online retailers tackled this obstacle by allowing shoppers to zoom in on products and "look inside" books. Free shipping opportunities from many retailers, including Amazon.com, likewise attracted buyers.

In time, people grew accustomed to online shopping, thanks in large part to Amazon.com as a leading retailer. Those initially nervous about entering personal and financial information online began to feel more secure. Now many shoppers are comfortable with "1-click" ordering.

Since its opening, Amazon.com continues expanding the variety of items it sells at competitive prices. It has grown into one of the largest online retailers in the world—but employees still use doors to make the desks in the offices.

Symptoms of online shopping addiction include feeling depressed if unable to shop online, lying about the amount of time and money one spends online, giving up social time in favor of shopping, and neglecting family and friends. Addicts also experience withdrawal symptoms when they are unable to access a computer, including irritability, anxiety, or emptiness.

Auction sites such as eBay are especially addicting for some shoppers. On auction sites, buyers experience a high when bidding. The rush of adrenaline from successfully outbidding others keeps shoppers going back for more. The purchased item itself is not necessarily important. As Young believes,

> eBay addicts will be there for the last few minutes of an online auction ready to outbid and bag the prize—"snipers" as they are called in eBay circles. It gets more serious when eBay addicts feel a sense of accomplishment when they are the highest bidder and begin to bid on items they don't need.[4]

Gambling

In 1980, before the rise of the Internet, Pathological Gambling, or gambling addiction, was first recognized as a disorder in the *DSM-3*. Internet addiction as a whole is most often compared to gambling addiction. It is no

Addicts crave the rush of 24-7 access to online gambling sites.

LEGAL ISSUES

In the United States, online gambling is technically illegal. A few states, such as New Jersey, allow online gambling within their borders. But federal law prohibits online gambling nationwide. US citizens are responsible for knowing and following the laws in their states.

The laws have affected the online gambling industry to some degree. Many US citizens follow the laws, and many former gambling sites now feature only games without real money.

But many gamblers, especially addicts, are not deterred. They gamble on sites operating outside the United States, or they gamble on illegal sites at their own risk.

surprise, then, that many people are addicted to online gambling.

The first online casino was launched in August 1996. Online gambling is now a multimillion dollar business, allowing people to join poker games, bet on sports, and play other games of chance without stepping foot in a casino.

In the United Kingdom in 2009, Justyn Larcombe made an online bet of roughly eight US dollars on a rugby match. It was only the beginning. He spent increasing amounts of time online, betting increasingly large sums of money. In a few years, his financial losses totaled well over $1 million. He lost his home, job, and car. He also lost his family—a wife and two young sons frustrated with his lifestyle. Larcombe eventually joined Gamblers Anonymous. Looking back, he realizes the bets had next to nothing to do with sports. "'I can't even remember who was playing. . . . Perhaps I was bored and wanted a thrill."[5]

For those with access to online gambling, the age group most at risk for addiction is teenagers. Brick-and-mortar casinos restrict access to anyone under legal gambling age. But online, proof of age is technically not required or can be fabricated. Teens with a troubled family life are the most likely to turn to online gambling as a means of dealing with depression, isolation, fears, and anxiety. Teens are not the only group that can develop online gambling addiction, however. Adults are also at risk, especially if they use online gambling as a stress release, such as after having a difficult day or arguing with someone.

People with online gambling addictions show classic symptoms. Addicts downplay their losses and exaggerate their winnings. Many online gamblers develop tolerance. They need to gamble more often and spend increasingly larger amounts of money to keep the desired high. Compulsive gamblers usually lie about their problem to friends and family. The anonymity of the Internet allows players to hide their addictions. The anonymity also disinhibits some people, leading them to gamble in ways they would not even at casinos.

Consequences of Spending Addictions

Like any form of Internet addiction, online shopping and online gambling become problems when they control individuals and interfere with life. When the behavior is a true addiction, people tend to isolate themselves from friends and family. Addicts are always thinking about going online to make their next bets or purchases. It is all they want to do, no matter the consequences of strained relationships and poor work or school performance.

In particular, addictive online shopping and gambling often lead to financial ruin. Unlike a gaming or social networking addiction, shopping and gambling addictions are based on spending. They often add up to serious debt. In the case of an eBay addiction, one woman drove herself $400,000 dollars in debt.[6] She also took out a second mortgage on her home and drained her savings account. When addicts run out of money to spend or bet, some turn to stealing, lying, or other illegal activities to feed the online addiction.

Individuals addicted to online shopping or gambling often lie about the financial consequences of their actions.

CHAPTER EIGHT

MEDIA MULTITASKING

Internet addicts get a rush from gaming, communicating, socializing, and spending—sometimes all at once. The Internet age brings multitasking to a new level. "At one time I can be banking, paying bills, checking my e-mail, Facebooking, e-mailing my parents, talking online to my friends, checking the TV Guide on the Internet, and researching possible graduate schools," one 22-year-old explained.[1] This behavior is known as media multitasking.

Having grown up with the Internet and all its capabilities, young people are most likely to media multitask. Donald Roberts, a professor of communication at Stanford, notes of his students, "It seems to me that there's almost a discomfort with not being stimulated."[2] For some people, young or old, the need for constant stimulation becomes an addiction.

With technology's many forms and functions, the possibilities for multitasking are endless.

Popcorn Brain

Edward M. Hallowell and John Ratey of Harvard have their own term for media-multitasking addiction: pseudo-attention deficit disorder. Other experts have coined a tongue-in-cheek name: online compulsive disorder. The name appropriately mimics obsessive-compulsive disorder, a recognized disorder in which individuals are driven to repeat certain behaviors that interfere with daily functioning.

Others describe it as "popcorn brain—a brain so accustomed to the constant stimulation of electronic multitasking that we're unfit for life offline, where things pop at a much slower pace."[3] How "unfit" some people are offline depends on how excessive their multitasking tends to be. Addicts may find themselves largely unable to function without being connected to everything at once.

Whatever this addiction is called, Hallowell says, "It's magnetic. . . . The more you touch it, the more you have to." As Ratey further explains, being multiwired can have a narcotic-like effect. "It's like a dopamine squirt to be connected. . . . It's an addiction."[4] For some, media multitasking can increase dopamine levels, producing the rush integral to any addiction. The rush is not only exciting, but it also creates a false sense of achievement. Addicts believe they accomplish so much when they multitask, when really their attention is scattered.

The Media-Multitasking Brain

Many media multitaskers—addicts and otherwise—claim they function best when juggling everything at once. But scientists disagree. Research has proven multitasking decreases focus and efficiency.

According to studies on multitasking, when an individual does more than one activity at a time, the brain must decide the order of the tasks and which task to do at any one moment. Focus and attention are divided into many pieces, affecting one's output and efficiency. As the number of tasks increases, efficiency deteriorates.

A 2007 study at Vanderbilt University had similar findings. The study determined multitasking leads to slower task completion and a greater number of errors. Researchers developed trials in which subjects were asked to perform a first task then a second with varying

DISTRACTED DRIVING

Media multitasking while driving can be dangerous for addicts and "normal" users alike. Mobile technology has increased distractions on the road, including talking on cell phones, texting, watching videos, and using navigation systems. Many drivers attempt all these tasks at once.

Of these activities, texting causes the most alarm. It requires an individual's eyes, hands, and brain power—all of which should be devoted to driving. To put it in perspective, texting takes a driver's eyes from the road for an average of 4.6 seconds. When traveling at 55 miles per hour (90 kmh), this is like driving an entire football field blind. Now 41 states have laws banning texting and driving, and 12 states prohibit the use of handheld devices.[5]

Multitasking behind the wheel forces the brain to prioritize a primary task over a secondary task. Accidents can happen when the brain makes a poor decision. As psychology professor Clifford Nass states:

When people are driving and talking on the phone or texting, that other task becomes what we call the primary task, the thing their brain focuses on. And driving becomes the sort of secondary . . . yeah, I'll pay attention when I want to [task].[6]

Texting while driving is a dangerous example of media multitasking.

amounts of time in between. The results revealed that
when the subjects were asked to perform two tasks
almost simultaneously, a traffic jam of sorts occurred
in the brain. Too much information processing at once
disallows people to multitask effectively.

Many Tasks, Many Consequences

For those addicted to media multitasking, what happens in their brains leads to serious consequences in real life. Those who text and drive—or even talk on a cell phone and drive—are at greater risk for accidents. Students who do homework while switching back and forth between text messages, music, and games frequently see decreased academic performance. Personal relationships suffer when family and friends must compete with tech gadgets for the addicts' attention.

Media-multitasking addicts often have difficulty managing their emotions. Hallowell and Ratey have noticed that media-multitasking addicts get frustrated when doing long-term activities demanding high levels of concentration. Researchers at Michigan State University have noted a connection between media multitasking and depression and anxiety. It is unclear whether multitasking leads to these disorders or whether people with these disorders are drawn to multitasking. But early research indicates a correlation worthy of more examination.

The Google Effect

Addicts see immediate consequences of media multitasking, such as impaired focus. But they may also face long-term consequences. Some experts note media multitasking trains young people's brains to access, manage, and process information quickly. But the tradeoff is it limits their ability to recall and comprehend that information. This potentially affects everything from the quality of their memories to their careers.

Many media multitaskers turn to Google and other search engines for instant access to information. But according to a 2011 study by Betsy Sparrow of Columbia,

YOUNG MULTITASKERS

Even young children are media multitaskers, with access to televisions, computers, tablets, and phones. According to the American Academy of Pediatrics, the average eight-year-old spends eight hours a day in front of screens of any sort. Among other consequences, overconsumption of technology can have adverse effects on health, including obesity.

The academy recommends no screen time at all for children under two and no more than two hours of entertainment-based screen time for older children.[7] Amidst the universal presence of technology, the academy recommends a balance, with parents setting clear rules for media use based on children's developmental needs.

Media multitasking from a young age may change the way the brain stores and accesses information.

the so-called Google Effect causes people to remember information differently:

> Our brains rely on the Internet for memory in much the same way they rely on the memory of a friend, family member or co-worker. We remember less through knowing information itself than by knowing where the information can be found.[8]

Further, Sparrow found people tend not to store in their own memory information easily accessed via the Internet. However, they are more likely to remember information not accessible online, such as personal histories or events.

Christine Rosen of the *New Atlantis* wrote that for digital natives "the great electronic din" is a part of life. For addicts, it consumes their lives. However, she cautions, "with crumbs of attention rationed out among many competing tasks, their culture may gain in information, but it will surely weaken in wisdom."[9]

Knowing young people are accustomed, if not addicted, to media multitasking, some educators have changed the way they teach. Many teachers and professors now use interactive websites, programs, blogs, discussion boards, and podcasts to capture their students' divided attention. Many times, students will access these learning tools all at once.

At a New Jersey high school, one teacher accepts that young people growing up in the digital age do not remember information. Instead, he contends, the Google Effect will lead media multitaskers down different career paths: "The world's going to require them to do stuff, to build things, to work on stuff." And as middle school principal Jason Levy asserts, "That's just the way the world is now."[10]

CHAPTER
NINE

SEEKING HELP

Technology—now available anytime, anywhere—has changed the world. It has redefined communication, interaction, and community. Digital natives know no other reality. In this new era, people of all ages are constantly learning how to define healthy, normal Internet use. But when people cross the line from use to abuse and even into addiction, they may benefit from the help of mental health professionals.

The Diagnosis

Approximately 86 percent of those supposedly addicted to the Internet are ultimately diagnosed with other disorders, such as depression, anxiety, or learning disabilities.[1] Perhaps some professionals choose other diagnoses because Internet addiction is not listed in the *DSM-5*. Choosing a diagnosis of a recognized disorder may help secure insurance coverage for treatment.

But perhaps the diagnoses reflect how for some individuals, Internet addiction is the manifestation of

---

Some Internet addicts seek professional help when they know they are no longer in control of their lives.

another disorder. For some, the Internet is a means to fuel other addictions, but it is not the root of an addiction in and of itself. The debate, then, is whether someone has an addiction to the Internet or has another addiction on the Internet.

For example, people with online gambling problems may not be addicted to the Internet at all, but simply addicted to gambling itself. Using the Internet is secondary. Or perhaps compulsive gamers suffer from anxiety and depression, which drives them to lose themselves in online games.

But since Young's research in the 1990s, many experts have declared Internet addiction is a legitimate diagnosis of its own accord. These professionals identify Internet use that results in self-destructive behavior, neurological

---

FUELING OTHER ADDICTIONS

Many experts contend the Internet is not the root of an addiction. Rather, the Internet fuels other addictions such as gambling and shopping. In parallel ways, it can also fuel an addiction to pornography, or sexually explicit images. Online, addicts can find instant and often free access to pornography, just as they can to gambling or shopping. With the complete anonymity the Internet allows, users can reduce the risk of getting caught, hide their addiction from loved ones, and shield themselves from some of the shame associated with the behavior.

problems, and psychological issues—all components of defined addiction.

Treatment

Recovery from any addiction can be a painful, personal journey. Each individual must find the path that works for him or her. This holds true for Internet addicts.

Ironically, there are online groups to help Internet addicts. One such group, On-Line Gamers Anonymous, holds daily online meetings and provides articles, message boards, references, and tips.

People with Internet addictions can also turn to software products that help monitor their online behaviors. These technological solutions hold people accountable by controlling their Internet use or by helping them maintain healthy levels of use. For example, compulsive shoppers can install a program that blocks all access to online stores.

For Internet addicts, there is also the question of whether to abstain from all online activities or whether to learn how to control online behavior. In comparison, people with other addictions often have the option to quit their problematic behavior outright. For instance, alcoholics can choose not to drink liquor, and gamblers

With the help of cognitive behavioral therapy, individuals learn to see their Internet use in new, healthier ways.

can choose not to enter casinos. But the problem for Internet addicts is that technology is so pervasive. How does one quit the Internet entirely? Can it even be done?

With abstaining from Internet technology being somewhat impractical, many therapists recommend cognitive behavioral therapy. This type of therapy focuses on changing thought and behavior processes.

With this approach, therapists first teach Internet addicts to modify the amount of time they spend online. Next, therapists help individuals address the denial and rationalizations they have used to justify their Internet use. Last, therapists help the individuals identify and treat other issues that may have fed the Internet addiction, such as depression or anxiety. By using this type of therapy, people can learn to self-monitor and balance their Internet use. Perhaps more important, they can learn to monitor the thoughts and feelings that may trigger compulsive online activity.

Treatment Centers

While Asia leads the way in developing treatment centers for Internet addiction, several centers now exist in the United States. In 1995, Young founded the Center for Internet Addiction to provide therapy sessions for those addicted to the Internet. She also opened a ten-day live-in treatment program in 2013 to help people with "digital detox."[2] Rather than expect people to stop using technology all together, the goal is to help them find a healthy balance in a technology-dependent society.

The reSTART Center, the first retreat program for Internet addiction, opened its doors in 2009. During a 45-day stay at reSTART, addicts unplug entirely and rediscover themselves during that Internet-free window. At the center, patients take on new responsibilities, enjoy cooking healthy meals, learn how to set boundaries around technology, and practice self-monitoring.

Realistically, one of the greatest obstacles for those interested in treatment programs is cost. Because Internet addiction is not recognized by the APA,

ADDRESSING DENIAL

Many addicts—of any kind—claim they do not have a problem. Therefore, a major component of any addiction treatment is addressing denial. To this end, experts at the reSTART Center help people overcome the denial surrounding their Internet addictions.

One compulsive gamer in the reSTART program said he did not understand why he had been so depressed. Another admitted to being in denial about his Internet gaming addiction even after it led him to drop out of college. "I didn't have to care about anything else," another said of using gaming to escape a socially awkward life.

These recovering addicts' stories reveal more than just denial, however. They also reveal a common element found in all addictions, whether chemical or behavioral: the fact that an addiction overtakes one's life. Or as Hilarie Cash, reSTART cofounder, states, any behavior becomes an addiction when "[you are] doing it to such an extent that it begins to control you rather than you being able to control it."[3]

At the reSTART Center, counselors help clients enjoy unplugged activities such as cooking.

insurance companies do not cover treatment. Thus, individuals must pay all expenses out of pocket. This can prevent some people from seeking the treatment they need. This financial reality is one of the reasons why experts are making steps to get Internet addiction officially recognized in future editions of the *DSM*.

Unplugging

In the age of ever-present technology, the line between Internet use and addiction is thin. Experts agree

PARENTS LEAD THE WAY

If parents wish to help children and teens avoid Internet addictions, one of the most effective means is to set limits and monitor usage. Most important, parents need to monitor their children's online activities and the amount of time they spend using technology.

Some experts also recommend parents set up their own profiles on Facebook or MySpace, watch YouTube videos, and generally surf the Internet to educate themselves about the current online experience. Parents also need to talk—and listen—about family members' expectations about Internet use.

everyone—even those without addictions—should unplug from technology for some time every day. The purpose of this practice is not to realize technology is bad, but to realize other activities are good.

For example, Hallowell of Harvard says playing video games does not "rot" one's brain. Instead, he says, "It's what you are not doing that's going to rot your life."[4] He feels wired people are missing out on other enriching opportunities. Unplugging from all computers, smartphones, tablets, and other gadgets a little bit every day will create time and space for the "real world" people are often missing out on. As Turkle states, "What technology makes easy is not always what nurtures the human spirit."[5]

Many experts specifically advocate for spending more time in nature to reset the brain. Research shows that a nature break both decreases stress and increases the ability to process information. When people focus on a natural environment, it requires using all five senses, which calms the brain.

Into the Future

The Internet was officially born in 1983, and it started becoming mainstream in the 1990s. The Internet went mobile in the 2000s. Now, how people communicate, socialize, learn, work, play, and spend have all changed because of the Internet. Who knows what new developments the digital future will hold.

But the revolution is too new and the technology changes too fast to fully define normal Internet use, let alone to define Internet addiction. However the condition is defined, and whether it is officially recognized, Internet addiction seems to be affecting individuals of all ages worldwide.

Hilarie Cash, cofounder of the reSTART Center, has been studying Internet addiction since the 1990s. "[I] had this sense back then that I was seeing the trickle before the flood," she said. "And the flood is upon us."[6]

TIMELINE

1952
Noughts and Crosses becomes the
first known video game.

1969
On October 29, the computer network project ARPANET
sends the first computer-to-computer communication.

1971
Engineer Ray Tomlinson sends the first e-mail.

1973
The first mobile phone call is made on April 3.

1983

The Internet is born on January 1.

1984

Motorola releases the first mobile
phone for public consumers.

1990

The World Wide Web is developed.

1992

The first text message is sent on December 3.

1995

Psychiatrist Ivan Goldberg posts a humorous
description of Internet addiction.

TIMELINE

1995
Kimberly Young opens the Center for Internet Addiction.

1995
Amazon.com launches on July 16.

1996
The first online casino is launched in August.

2004
On February 4, Facebook is founded.

2009
The reSTART Center opens its doors.

2010
In March, a couple in South Korea uses Internet addiction as a defense in the death of their baby daughter.

2011
The Google Effect study reveals search engines have changed human memory.

2013
The *DSM-5* marks Internet Gaming Disorder for further study but does not recognize Internet addiction.

ESSENTIAL FACTS

At Issue

- The boom of the Internet began in the early 1990s. By the mid-1990s, mental health professionals began questioning whether Internet addiction was emerging.

- In 2010, a South Korean couple was cleared of causing their baby's death due to Internet addiction.

- The American Psychiatric Association (APA) did not recognize Internet addiction as a disorder in its 2013 *Diagnostic and Statistical Manual of Mental Disorders* (*DSM*).

- Despite the APA's stance, 2013 surveys indicated as much as 8.2 percent of the population may be affected by Internet addiction.

Critical Dates

1960s to 1990s

Beginning in the 1960s, the earliest forms of Internet use developed. January 1, 1983, marked the official birthday of the Internet. By the early 1990s, the World Wide Web made the Internet easier to use and more popular.

1995 to 2013

As early as 1995, the concept of Internet addiction emerged as an area of study and treatment. In the new millennium, Internet use exploded worldwide. In particular, mobile technology allowed people to access information and communicate on the go.

2013 to present

The APA published its *DSM-5* but did not list Internet addiction as a mental disorder. The subset of Internet Gaming Disorder was marked for more study. But with Internet use nearly universal for teens and most adults, overuse sometimes blurs into abuse. A number of professionals push for Internet addiction to be recognized as an official mental disorder.

Quote

"Technology appeals to us most where we are most vulnerable. And we are vulnerable. We're lonely, but we're afraid of intimacy. And so from social networks to sociable robots, we're designing technologies that will give us the illusion of companionship without the demands of friendship."—*Sheryl Turkle, sociologist and psychologist*

GLOSSARY

censored
To be altered, deleted, or banned.

digital native
Someone who grew up with digital technology as a part of everyday life.

guild
A small community of players who play online games together.

modem
A device that changes the form of electric signals so information can be sent between computers via telephone lines.

netizen

An active Internet user; a combination of the words *net* and *citizen*.

network

A system of computers and other devices connected to one another.

neurotransmitter

A chemical substance that transmits impulses across synapses in the brain.

ADDITIONAL RESOURCES

Selected Bibliography

The Center for Internet Addiction. *Net Addiction*. The Center for Internet Addiction, 2009–2013. Web. 5 Mar. 2014.

Pew Research Center. *Pew Research Internet Project*. Pew Research Center, 2014. Web. 5 Mar. 2014.

Roberts, Kevin. *Cyber Junkie*. Center City, MN: Hazelden. 2010. Print.

Rosen, Larry D. *iDisorder*. New York: Palgrave Macmillan, 2012. Print.

Turkle, Sherry. *Alone Together—Why We Expect More from Technology and Less from Each Other*. New York: Basic, 2011. Print.

Watkins, S. Craig. *The Young and the Digital*. Boston: Beacon, 2009. Print.

Further Readings

Anderson, M. T. *Feed*. Cambridge, MA: Candlewick, 2012. Print.

Louv, Richard. *Last Child in the Woods: Saving Our Children from Nature-Deficit Disorder*. Chapel Hill, NC: Algonquin Books of Chapel Hill, 2008. Print.

Willard, Nancy E. *Cyber-Safe Kids, Cyber-Savvy Teens: Helping Young People Learn to Use the Internet Safely and Responsibly*. San Francisco: Jossey-Bass, 2007. Print.

Websites

To learn more about Essential Issues, visit **booklinks.abdopublishing.com.** These links are routinely monitored and updated to provide the most current information available.

For More Information

For more information on this subject, contact or visit the following organizations:

Computer History Museum
1401 North Shoreline Blvd
Mountain View, CA 94043
650-810-1010
http://www.computerhistory.org/internet_history
The museum reveals each step in the technology revolution, from the very first computers to today's digital explosion.

reSTART Center
1001 290th Avenue SE
Fall City, WA 98024-7403
800-682-6934
http://netaddictionrecovery.com
At the reSTART Center, people struggling with Internet addiction learn to unplug and find themselves in a peaceful retreat environment.

SOURCE NOTES

Chapter 1. Lost in the Digital World

1. Bryce J. Renninger. "Will You See This Movie? Sundance Alum Directs Doc about First Successful Internet Addiction Manslaughter Defense." *Indiewire*. A SnagFilms Company, 9 October 2012. Web. 2 Apr. 2014.

2. Sangwon Yoon. "Internet Addicts Guilty of Starving Baby to Death While Tending to Virtual Child." *Huff Post–Tech*. TheHuffingtonPost.com, 28 May 2010. Web. 2 Apr. 2014.

3. Choe Sang-Hun. "A Fantasy World Is Creating Problems in South Korea." *New York Times*. New York Times, 26 May 2010. Web. 2 Apr. 2014.

4. Frances Cha. "10 Things South Korea Does Better Than Anywhere Else." *CNN Travel*. Cable News Network, 27 Nov. 2013. Web. 2 Apr. 2014.

5. Douglas Main. "Digital Natives: The Most & Least Wired Countries Revealed." *Live Science*. TechMedia Network, 11 Oct. 2013. Web. 2 Apr. 2014.

6. Michael Dhar. "Psychiatry's Contested Bible: How the New DSM Treats Addiction." *Pacific Standard*. Pacific Standard, 2 May 2013. Web. 2 Apr. 2014.

7. Hilarie Cash, et al. "Internet Addiction: A Brief Summary of Research and Practice." *US National Library of Medicine*. National Center for Biotechnology Information, Nov. 2012. Web. 2 Apr. 2014.

Chapter 2. Origins of the Internet

1. S. Craig Watkins. *The Young and the Digital*. Boston: Beacon, 2009. Print. 1.

2. Ibid. 3.

3. Thom File. "Computer and Internet Use in the United States." *United States Census Bureau*. US Department of Commerce, May 2013. Web. 2 Apr. 2014.

4. "Trend Data (Adults)." *Pew Internet*. Pew Internet & American Life Project, May 2013. Web. 2 Apr. 2014.

5. "Trend Data (Teens)." *Pew Internet*. Pew Internet & American Life Project, Sept. 2012. Web. 2 Apr. 2014.

6. "5 Major Moments in Cellphone History." *CBC News–Technology and Science*. CBC–Radio Canada, 3 Apr. 2013. Web. 2 Apr. 2014.

7. Will Shanklin. "2012 Smartphone Comparison Guide." *Gizmag*. Gizmag, 7 Nov. 2012. Web. 2 Apr. 2014.

8. Joanna Brenner. "Pew Internet: Mobile." *Pew Internet*. Pew Internet & American Life Project, 18 Sept. 2013. Web. 2 Apr. 2014.

9. Joanna Stern. "Happy 20th Birthday, Text Message, but You're Past Your Prime." *ABC News*. ABC News Internet Ventures, 3 Dec. 2012. Web. 2 Apr. 2014.

10. Maeve Duggan. "Cell Phone Activities 2013." *Pew Internet*. Pew Internet & American Life Project, 19 Sept. 2013. Web. 2 Apr. 2014.

11. Kathryn Zickuhr and Aaron Smith. "Digital Differences." *Pew Internet*. Pew Internet & American Life Project, 13 Apr. 2012. Web. 2 Apr. 2014.

12. Mary Madden, et al. "Teens and Technology 2013." *Pew Internet*. Pew Internet & American Life Project, 13 Mar. 2013. Web. 2 Apr. 2014.

Chapter 3. Internet Addiction Emerges

1. David Wallis. "Just Click No." *New Yorker*. Condé Nast, 13 Jan. 1997. Web. 2 Apr. 2014.

2. Joel Best and Scott R. Harris, eds. *Making Sense of Social Problems*. Boulder, CO: Lynne Rienner, 2013. Print. 198–199.

3. Kimberly S. Young and Cristiano Nabuco de Abreu, eds. *Internet Addiction: A Handbook and Guide to Evaluation and Treatment*. Hoboken, NJ: Wiley, 2011. Print. 6.

4. "Interview with Dr. David Greenfield on Internet and Video Game Addiction." *YouTube*. YouTube, Mar. 2008. Web. 2 Apr. 2014.

5. Justin W. Patchin. "Summary of Our Research (2004–2013)." *Cyberbullying Research Center*. Cyberbullying Research Center, 10 July 2013. Web. 2 Apr. 2014.

6. Sameer Hinduja, PhD, and Justin W. Patchin, PhD. "Fact Sheet: Cyberbullying Identification, Prevention and Response." *Cyberbullying Research Center*. Cyberbullying Research Center, n.d. Web. 2 Apr. 2014.

7. Joel Best and Scott R. Harris, eds. *Making Sense of Social Problems*. Boulder, CO: Lynne Rienner, 2013. Print. 206.

Chapter 4. Gaming

1. Kevin Roberts. *Cyber Junkie*. Center City, MN: Hazelden. 2010. Print. 4.

2. Anne Hiller. "Internet Gaming Disorder Fact Sheet." *DSM-5 Development*. American Psychiatric Association, 16 May 2013. Web. 7 Apr. 2014.

3. Caroline Fairchild. "Gamification Nation." *CNN Money*. Cable News Network, 9 Dec. 2013. Web. 2 Apr. 2014.

4. S. Craig Watkins. *The Young and the Digital*. Boston: Beacon, 2009. Print. 116–117.

5. John D. Sutter. "'StarCraft' and 'Warcraft' Makers Take on Gaming Addiction." *CNN Tech*. Cable News Network, 6 Aug. 2012. Web. 2 Apr. 2014.

6. Kevin Roberts. *Cyber Junkie*. Center City, MN: Hazelden. 2010. Print. 125.

7. Jaime Holguin. "Uncle Sam Wants Video Gamers." *CBS Evening News*. CBS Interactive, 8 Feb. 2005. Web. 2 Apr. 2014.

8. "Video Games and Gaming Addiction." *Net Addiction*. Center for Internet Addiction Recovery, n.d. Web. 2 Apr. 2014.

9. Cam Adair. "Escaping Video Game Addiction." *Kingpin Social*. Kingpin Social Dynamics, Sept. 2013. Web. 2 Apr. 2014.

Chapter 5. Communicating

1. Masuma Ahuja. "Teens Are Spending More Time Consuming Media, on Mobile Devices." *Washington Post Live*. Washington Post, 13 Mar. 2013. Web. 2 Apr. 2014.

2. "Dr. David Greenfield on Early Show." *YouTube*. YouTube, Sept. 2010. Web. 2 Apr. 2014.

3. Joanna Brenner. "Pew Internet: Mobile." *Pew Internet*. Pew Internet & American Life Project, 18 Sept. 2013. Web. 2 Apr. 2014.

4. Nancy Gibbs. "Your Life Is Fully Mobile." *Time Tech*. Time, 16 Aug. 2012. Web. 2 Apr. 2014.

5. "Young People Completely Wedded to Their Mobile Phones." *MarketingCharts*. Watershed Publishing, 14 Dec. 2012. Web. 2 Apr. 2014.

6. Joanna Brenner. "Pew Internet: Mobile." *Pew Internet*. Pew Internet & American Life Project, 18 Sept. 2013. Web. 2 Apr. 2014.

SOURCE NOTES CONTINUED

7. Patrick Thibodeau. "Cellphone Vibration Syndrome and Other Signs of Tech Addiction." *ComputerWorld*. ComputerWorld, 24 May 2012. Web. 2 Apr. 2014.

8. Dale Archer. "Smartphone Addiction." *Psychology Today*. Sussex Publishers, 25 July 2013. Web. 2 Apr. 2014.

9. Vicky Kung. "Rise of 'Nomophobia': More People Fear Loss of Mobile Contact." *CNN Tech*. Cable News Network, 7 Mar. 2012. Web. 2 Apr. 2014.

10. Amanda Lenhart. "Teens, Smartphones & Texting." *Pew Internet*. Pew Internet & American Life Project, 19 Mar. 2012. Web. 2 Apr. 2014.

11. Joanna Brenner. "Pew Internet: Mobile." *Pew Internet*. Pew Internet & American Life Project, 18 Sept. 2013. Web. 2 Apr. 2014.

12. Amanda Lenhart. "Teens and Sexting." *Pew Internet*. Pew Internet & American Life Project, 15 Dec. 2009. Web. 2 Apr. 2014.

13. Larry D. Rosen, PhD. *iDisorder*. New York: Palgrave Macmillan, 2012. Print. 123.

Chapter 6. Social Networking

1. Joanna Brenner. "Pew Internet: Social Networking (Full Detail)." *Pew Internet*. Pew Internet & American Life Project, 5 Aug. 2013. Web. 2 Apr. 2014.

2. Janna Anderson and Lee Rainie. "Millennials Will Benefit and Suffer Due to Their Hyperconnected Lives." *Pew Internet*. Pew Internet & American Life Project, 29 Feb. 2012. Web. 2 Apr. 2014.

3. Ibid.

4. Mary Madden, et al. "Teens, Social Media, and Privacy." *Pew Internet*. Pew Internet & American Life Project, 21 May 2013. Web. 2 Apr. 2014.

5. Janna Anderson and Lee Rainie. "Millennials Will Benefit and Suffer Due to Their Hyperconnected Lives." *Pew Internet*. Pew Internet & American Life Project, 29 Feb. 2012. Web. 2 Apr. 2014.

6. S. Craig Watkins. *The Young and the Digital*. Boston: Beacon, 2009. Print. 67.

7. "Photo and Video Sharing Grow Online." *Pew Internet*. Pew Internet & American Life Project, 28 Oct. 2013. Web. 2 Apr. 2014.

8. S. Craig Watkins. *The Young and the Digital*. Boston: Beacon, 2009. Print. 133.

9. Sherry Turkle. "Connected, but Alone?" *TED*. TED Conferences, Mar. 2012. Web. 2 Apr. 2014.

10. "Online Dating & Relationships." *Pew Internet*. Pew Internet & American Life Project, 21 Oct. 2013. Web. 2 Apr. 2014.

11. Sherry Turkle. "Connected, but Alone?" *TED*. TED Conferences, Mar. 2012. Web. 2 Apr. 2014.

12. Katie Hafner. "To Deal with Obsession, Some Defriend Facebook." *New York Times*. New York Times, 20 Dec. 2009. Web. 2 Apr. 2014.

Chapter 7. Shopping and Gambling

1. Amanda M. Fairbanks. "Gilt Addicts Anonymous: The Daily Online Flash Sale Fixation." *Huff Post–Women*. TheHuffingtonPost.com, 22 Dec. 2011. Web. 2 Apr. 2014.

2. Daniel Bortz. "Confessions of Former Shopaholics." *MONEY–Personal Finance*. US News & World Report, 25 Jan. 2013. Web. 2 Apr. 2014.

3. Amanda M. Fairbanks. "Gilt Addicts Anonymous: The Daily Online Flash Sale Fixation." *Huff Post–Women*. TheHuffingtonPost.com, 22 Dec. 2011. Web. 2 Apr. 2014.

4. Mark Griffiths, Ph.D. "In Excess-Gambling, Gaming and Extreme Behavior." *Psychology Today*. Sussex Publishers, 11 Aug. 2013. Web. 2 Apr. 2014.

5. Alice A. Jarvis. "A Terrifying Parable of the Addictive Power of Internet Gambling." *Mail Online–News*. Daily Mail, 16 Aug. 2013. Web. 2 Apr. 2014.

6. "Take Our eBay Addiction Quiz." *Net Addiction*. Center for Internet Addiction Recovery, n.d. Web. 2 Apr. 2014.

Chapter 8. Media Multitasking

1. S. Craig Watkins. *The Young and the Digital*. Boston: Beacon, 2009. Print. 164–165.

2. Claudia Wallis. "genM: The Multitasking Generation." *Time*. Time, 27 Mar. 2006. Web. 2 Apr. 2014.

3. Elizabeth Cohen. "Does Life Online Give You 'Popcorn Brain'?" *CNN Health*. Cable News Network, 23 June 2011. Web. 2 Apr. 2014.

4. Barbara Bartlein. "The Addiction of Multitasking." *CareerIntelligence*. CareerIntelligence, 24 Jan. 2014. Web. 2 Apr. 2014.

5. "Distraction.gov." *Distraction.gov*. National Highway Traffic Safety Administration, n.d. Web. 2 Apr. 2014.

6. "The Myth of Multitasking." *NPR*. NPR, 10 May 2013. Web. 2 Apr. 2014.

7. Tia Ghose. "Pediatricians: No More than 2 Hours Screen-Time Daily for Kids." *Scientific American*. Scientific American, 28 Oct. 2013. Web. 2 Apr. 2014.

8. "Study Finds That Memory Works Differently in the Age of Google." *Research*. Columbia University, 14 July 2011. Web. 2 Apr. 2014.

9. S. Craig Watkins. *The Young and the Digital*. Boston: Beacon, 2009. Print. 169.

10. *Digital Nation*. Rachel Dretzin, prod. and dir. FRONTLINE and Ark Media, 2010. DVD.

Chapter 9. Seeking Help

1. S. Craig Watkins. *The Young and the Digital*. Boston: Beacon, 2009. Print. 135.

2. Liz Neporent. "Hospital First in US to Treat Internet Addiction." *ABC News*. ABC News Internet Ventures, 4 Sept. 2013. Web. 2 Apr. 2014.

3. "When Playing Video Games Means Sitting on Life's Sidelines." *NPR*. NPR, 20 Oct. 2013. Web. 2 Apr. 2014.

4. Claudia Wallis. "genM: The Multitasking Generation." *Time*. Time, 27 Mar. 2006. Web. 2 Apr. 2014.

5. "Speakers Sherry Turkle: Cultural Analyst." *TED*. TED Conferences, n.d. Web. 2 Apr. 2014.

6. "When Playing Video Games Means Sitting on Life's Sidelines." *NPR*. NPR, 20 Oct. 2013. Web. 2 Apr. 2014.

INDEX

ABOUT THE AUTHOR

Laura Perdew is a digital immigrant, author, and former middle school teacher. She writes fiction and nonfiction for children of all ages, including numerous titles for the education market and a guide for parents traveling through Colorado with small children (*Kids on the Move! Colorado*). She lives and plays in Boulder, Colorado, with her husband and twin digital-native boys.

ABOUT THE CONSULTANT

Dr. Keith Beard received his doctorate in clinical psychology from Wright State University in Dayton, Ohio. He is currently a professor of psychology and the director of the psychology clinic at Marshall University in Huntington, West Virginia. In addition to teaching, he is a licensed psychologist and a licensed professional counselor. He has a small private psychotherapy practice, does consulting work, and leads organizational workshops. He is a member of the American Psychological Association and the West Virginia Psychological Association. His research interests include Internet addiction, psychological factors in technology and media, men's issues, humor in teaching, and religion and psychology.